AUG - - 2023

NATIONAL
GEOGRAPHIC
KiDS

CAN'T GET ENOUGH

HORSE Stuff

FUN FACTS, AWESOME INFO, COOL GAMES, SILLY JOKES, AND MORE!

NEIL CAVANAUGH

NATIONAL GEOGRAPHIC
WASHINGTON, D.C.

TABLE OF
CONTENTS

GIDDYUP, LET'S GO!

From carrying knights into battle to dancing across arenas in time to music, horses have shared the world with humans for thousands of years. We gave them hay and carrots. They carried us around on their backs. We took them to doctors and to get new shoes. They pulled our wagons. Somewhere along the way, though, we became more than just co-workers. We brush their coats and braid their manes, and we give them their favorite treats because we love them.

Looking to fill your knowledge stable? You've got the right book in hand. Inside, you'll find more horse facts than you can shake a crop at. You'll use your horse sense to tackle trivia questions, matching games, and word scrambles. Wild horses won't be able to drag you away from hilarious horse jokes or fun activities that will help you discover exciting things about your favorite equines. Read stories from horse experts and horse enthusiasts, and take part in the adventures of thoroughbreds and pit ponies.

Saddle up! It's time to head down the old, dusty trail.

HORSES AND PONIES ARE THE SAME SPECIES: *EQUUS CABALLUS.* THE MAIN DIFFERENCE IS HEIGHT: PONIES ARE UP TO 58 INCHES (147 CM) TALL; HORSES ARE OVER 58 INCHES TALL.

HORSE HUMOR

Q What do horses say when they fall down?

A "Help! I've fallen and I can't giddy-up."

Q What do horses use to make a sandwich?

A Thorough-bread.

Q What did the mother horse say to her foal?

A It's pasture bedtime.

TONGUE TWISTER

SAY THIS FAST THREE TIMES:

One-One was a racehorse.
Two-Two was one, too.
One-One won one race.
Two-Two won one, too.

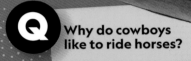

Q Why do cowboys like to ride horses?

A Because the horses are too heavy to carry.

PONY: Doctor, I feel sick. I have a terrible sore throat.

DOCTOR: It's OK. You're just a little hoarse.

Q You're riding a horse at full speed, a giraffe is right beside you, and a lion is nipping at your heels. What do you do?

A Get off the carousel.

RIDDLE ME THIS ...

Q What do you call a horse that likes to stay up late?

A A night mare.

HORSES IN OUR LANGUAGE

Horses and humans have lived and worked together for thousands of years. Even if you have never seen a horse in person, they might show up in the way you speak. Plenty of the words we use come from our history with horses. See if you can match the following phrases with the correct definition. Write your answers (numbered 1 through 11) on a separate piece of paper. Then compare them to the answer key at the bottom of the page.

1 CHOMP AT THE BIT

2 DARK HORSE

3 DON'T LOOK A GIFT HORSE IN THE MOUTH

4 GET OFF YOUR HIGH HORSE

5 HORSE OF A DIFFERENT COLOR

6 LONG IN THE TOOTH

7 ONE-HORSE TOWN

8 PUT THE CART BEFORE THE HORSE

9 STRAIGHT FROM THE HORSE'S MOUTH

10 TROJAN HORSE

11 YOU CAN LEAD A HORSE TO WATER, BUT YOU CANNOT MAKE IT DRINK

A You can give someone an opportunity to do something, but you cannot force them to do it.

B A small or less noticeable place

C Old

D Stop acting like you are better than everyone else

E A person or thing that is different or unique

F Something intended to secretly bring about the downfall of an opponent

G A competitor about whom little is known who unexpectedly wins

H Information from a reliable source

I To be restlessly impatient to do something

J Do not criticize something that has been given as a gift.

K To do things out of order or get ahead of yourself

MEASURING UP

Equines come in all shapes and sizes, from tall and skinny to small and powerful. Want to find out how different breeds measure up? Take a look at the weight of these breeds compared to popular objects that match their size.

A MINI HORSE CANNOT BE MORE THAN 38 INCHES (97 CM) TALL AT THE WITHERS.

Shetland Pony

WEIGHT: 440 pounds (200 kg)

THAT'S ABOUT AS HEAVY AS: A riding lawn mower

Thoroughbred

WEIGHT: 1,000 pounds (454 kg)

THAT'S ABOUT AS HEAVY AS: Four full-size refrigerators

Belgian Draft

WEIGHT: 2,200 pounds (1,000 kg)

THAT'S ABOUT AS HEAVY AS: A baby humpback whale

Welsh Pony

WEIGHT: 750 pounds (340 kg)

THAT'S ABOUT AS HEAVY AS: Four adult male red kangaroos

WHICH HORSE BREED MATCHES YOUR PERSONALITY?

Horses come in all shapes, sizes, and personalities. Which horse is most like you? Pick the best answer but choose only one for each question. Write down the letter of your answers on a piece of paper, then add up your score to discover your ideal stablemate. And remember, if these descriptions don't fit you, that's OK! This quiz is just for fun!

1. You are heading out for a meal. What type of restaurant will you go to?

a. I am up for anything.

b. I love fast food.

c. Whatever the rest of my family wants is fine with me.

d. I would prefer a light snack.

e. I would rather stay home and make myself some dinner.

2. If you were to spend a vacation at a lakeside resort, which activity would you prefer to do?

a. I would water-ski over and over again.

b. I would ride a Jet Ski.

c. I would relax on a pontoon boat big enough for my whole family.

d. I would lie in the sun on the beach.

e. I would jump in the water and go for a swim.

3. What Olympic event would you most like to compete in?

a. gymnastics

b. luge

c. any team sport

d. weight lifting

e. mountain biking

4. You're locked in a room. What do you do?

a. Wait patiently for someone to let me out.

b. Knock the door down.

c. Write a letter to my best friend telling them about my adventure.

d. Yell out the window for help.

e. It doesn't matter. No room could hold me!

5. What is your favorite way to travel?

a. train   d. dogsled

b. plane   e. boat

c. RV

6. What is your favorite season?

a. fall

b. summer

c. all of them

d. winter

e. spring

7. You're taking a quiz at school. Which sounds more like you?

a. I calmly complete the questions, one after another.

b. I hurry up and complete the questions so I can be the first one done.

c. I look around for a friend to chat with.

d. I don't believe in tests.

e. Quiz? I've already left for recess.

8. Pick a new after-school activity!

a. ballroom dancing

b. jet-pack racing

c. flash mob

d. powerlifting

e. camping

CHECK YOUR SCORE. Count up how many of each letter you have chosen. Then read the results below. If you have a tie score, read the results for both letters:

Three or more a's:
You are most like a Tennessee Walking Horse.
The TWH is known for its calm demeanor and its silky-smooth ride. This breed was originally used as an all-purpose horse on farms in Tennessee. No matter how rocky the terrain, they remain sure-footed. This horse walks with a distinctive gait. It keeps one hoof on the ground as it moves.

Three or more b's:
You are most like a Thoroughbred.
Like a Thoroughbred, you are highly competitive and driven to succeed. You both like to go fast! While it can occasionally flash a silly side, this horse has a solid work ethic and boundless energy. They would much rather be busy with a task than sit around bored.

Three or more c's:
You are most like a Morgan horse.
Known for making excellent companions and acting friendly to everyone, this horse is the golden retriever of the horse world. The other horses would probably vote it "Most Likely to Cuddle Up With Its Owner and Watch a Movie." Morgans cooperate well and aim to please.

Three or more d's: You are most like a Shetland pony.
They were used in coal mines because they can fit in small spaces while still hauling considerable loads (up to double their body weight). Shetland ponies do well in cold climates because they have a double coat. Known for being highly intelligent and a little stubborn, they also have a gentle nature.

Three or more e's (or not three or more of anything):
You are most like a mustang.
Like the mustang, you are independent and able to fend for yourself. This breed has survived predators, rugged terrain, and harsh weather. These animals are known for paying close attention to their surroundings and for being quick learners.

WILD & FREE

Before horses were domesticated by humans, they were wild animals. They lived in herds, slept under the stars, and grazed on any vegetation they could find. Around 6,000 years ago, humans began breeding horses for different tasks, including travel and herding. As time went on, most horses remained domesticated. But not all of them! Several horse breeds still live wild and free.

Sable Island

Sable Island horses are native to Canada. In 1961, a law was passed to protect the island's ecosystem. The herd of about 500 horses lives freely, and humans are not allowed within 66 feet (20 m) of them.

NORTH AMERICA
Western U.S.A.

Sable Island, CANADA

PACIFIC OCEAN

ATLANTIC OCEAN

SOUTH AMERICA

Mustang

Mustang is the name given to feral horses in North America. They descend from horses that explorers brought to the Americas roughly 500 years ago.

Przewalski's
The Przewalski's horse, native to central Asia, may be the only true wild horse breed.

ARCTIC OCEAN

ASIA

MONGOLIA

Southern **FRANCE** **EUROPE**

AFRICA

INDIAN OCEAN

PACIFIC OCEAN

NAMIBIA

AUSTRALIA

SOUTHERN OCEAN

ANTARCTICA

SCIENTISTS CALL HORSES "FERAL" IF THEIR ANCESTORS WERE DOMESTICATED AND THE HORSES THEN ESCAPED BACK INTO THE WILD.

Namib Desert
In the Garub Plains in Namibia in southwest Africa, a group of feral horses has survived in desert conditions for nearly 100 years. These Namib Desert horses have adapted to be able to go up to 72 hours without water! There are only about 100 to 150 of them today, and they are Africa's only feral horse breed.

Camargue
The Camargue horse is native to southern France. They are descendants of the Solutré horse of the Stone Age, making them one of the world's most ancient breeds! Standing around 52 inches (132 cm) tall, the Camargue has a whitish-gray coat and feet specially adapted for standing in water.

PRZEWALSKI'S HORSE

THE PRZEWALSKI'S (SHUH-VAL-SKEEZ) HORSE,

often referred to as a P-horse for short, is considered the last "wild" horse. At one time, scientists thought all horses were descended from P-horses, but they have since disproved that theory. Both horses and P-horses are descended from a common ancestor that lived about 500,000 years ago. The horse and P-horse have been cousins ever since.

NOT QUITE A HORSE

The P-horse looks like a domesticated horse, except that its mane sticks up instead of lying flat, and it has no forelock, which is the part of the mane that hangs over the forehead. It is also shorter than a horse and has a bigger head, a thicker neck, and a wider belly. Most of its body is tan, but its legs are a darker shade of brown, which makes it look as if it is wearing knee socks.

The P-horse typically lives in family groups with one stallion, up to three mares, and their offspring. Multiple family groups form a herd. Stallions that haven't yet found mates often live together in bachelor herds.

HANGING IN THERE

The P-horse went extinct in the wild in the 1960s, with the last P-horses observed in the Gobi desert in Mongolia. Fortunately, even though no P-horses remained in the wild, a few survived in zoos. Scientists around the world worked together to help the P-horses reproduce. They were successful enough that, beginning in the 1990s, P-horses were set free in wildlife refuges in China, Kazakhstan, Mongolia, and Russia.

THE P-HORSE IS THE NATIONAL ANIMAL OF MONGOLIA. MONGOLIANS CALL THE P-HORSE *TAKHI*, WHICH MEANS "SPIRIT."

IN THE LATE 1950s, ONLY 12 P-HORSES EXISTED. TODAY, CLOSE TO 2,000 P-HORSES LIVE IN CAPTIVITY AND IN THE WILD.

BOTH HORSES AND P-HORSES SHARE A COMMON ANCESTOR WITH THE RHINOCEROS.

FOAL FUN

A FOAL IS A BABY HORSE THAT'S LESS THAN ONE YEAR OLD.

DURING ITS FIRST THREE MONTHS, A FOAL SLEEPS 12 HOURS PER DAY. ADULT HORSES TYPICALLY SLEEP ONLY ABOUT THREE HOURS PER DAY.

MOST FOALS START EATING SOLID FOODS—GRASS AND HAY—WITHIN A WEEK OF BIRTH.

When a **FOAL** is born, its hooves are covered with soft tissue to protect its mother's uterus and birth canal.

A growing foal can gain up to three pounds (1.4 kg) a day.

When a foal is born, its legs are already 80 to 90 percent of their adult length.

As prey animals, foals need to quickly learn to run to escape danger. Most foals can stand within one hour of birth, walk in five hours, and canter within **24 hours.**

A **male foal** is called a **colt;** a **female foal** is a **filly.**

Within a week of being born, foals can drink up to 25 percent of their body weight in milk (usually from their mother) each day.

HORSE HUMOR

Q What did the hungry Appaloosa say when he finished his hay?

A That hit the spots.

Q How much money does a bronco have?

A A buck.

Q When does a horse go to sleep at night?

A Whinny wants to.

CHRISTIE: Did you hear about Kendall? He ate six plastic horses.

OMAR: Oh no! Is he OK?

CHRISTIE: Yup. The doctor described his condition as "stable."

Q What do you give a horse with a cold?

A Cough stirrup.

TONGUE TWISTER

SAY THIS FAST THREE TIMES:
Thirty-three thirsty, thundering thoroughbreds thumped Mr. Thurber on Thursday.

Q What team of horses travel all around the world?

A The Globe Trotters.

MAGIC FLIGHT · **BROADWAY** · AIRLINE NORTH · ZURICH · LONDON · ITALIA · California · BERLIN · Netherlands Airlines · UNITED AIR LINES

THE EYE-POPPING TRUTH ABOUT HOW HORSES SEE

A HORSE HAS TWO AREAS AROUND ITS BODY WHERE IT CANNOT SEE: RIGHT IN FRONT OF ITS NOSE AND A FEW FEET DIRECTLY BEHIND ITS TAIL.

HORSES HAVE THE LARGEST EYES OF ANY LAND MAMMAL.

HORSES ARE PREY ANIMALS.

To protect themselves from predators such as mountain lions and wolves, horses rely on their speed. But horses have to catch sight of these predators first. Fortunately, a horse's eyes are very good at seeing that danger is approaching.

EYES (ALMOST) IN THE BACK OF ITS HEAD

You have two eyes that are both on the front of your head. Your eyes are great at showing what is in front of you but not at showing what is on either side of you. When you stand in the middle of a room and look straight ahead, the area you can see is called your field of vision. You can turn your head or twist your body to see other parts of the room, but you can't see it all at the same time.

A horse also has two eyes, but they are on either side of its head. If a horse were in the middle of the same room, it could see almost the whole area at once. This bigger field of vision makes it very easy for the horse to see if anything scary is nearby.

PROCESSING POWER

You have two eyes, but they work as one. Your brain takes the image from your left eye and the image from your right eye and combines them into a single picture. That combined picture is what you see. A horse's eyes operate separately. Its left eye can watch the sunset, while its right eye watches you bring it a carrot. And, unlike the human brain, its brain can see both images at once.

PONY POWER!

STRONGEST

SHETLAND PONY

In the mid-19th century, thousands of Shetland ponies were brought from the Shetland Islands off the coast of Scotland to England to work in coal mines. Shetlands are the smallest breed of British pony and can pull twice their weight, so they were the ideal animal for this difficult labor.

MOST LIKELY TO SING IN THE RAIN

EXMOOR PONY

Hailing from England, where rainfall is frequent, the Exmoor pony evolved to cope with getting wet. It has a "toad eye," which is extra flesh above and below its eyes that helps keep out water. In the winter, the Exmoor also has two coats. The top coat is made of long oily hairs that keep the inner coat dry. The pony also has a fan of short coarse hairs at the dock, or top, of its tail, which allows water to run down its legs instead of soaking its underbelly.

HACKNEY PONY

Before the invention of the car, Hackney ponies pulled carriages. In addition to being strong, the Hackney walks in an animated way, lifting its knees high in the air. Today, they are best known as harness ponies, competing in shows where they pull carriages at different speeds around the ring.

BEST
JUMPER

CONNEMARA PONY

According to legend, when the Spanish Armada ran aground off the Irish coast in 1588, Andalusian horses escaped the ships and mated with the native Irish ponies, creating the Connemara. Over time, Ireland's rocky terrain helped the Connemara become sure-footed travelers. Today, they compete at international levels in show jumping.

ESOPHAGUS
The esophagus is a muscular tube in the throat that allows food to travel from the mouth to the stomach.

MOUTH
Digestion starts in the horse's mouth. Its teeth tear food into little pieces and mix it with saliva, which has chemicals that break down the food.

STOMACH
A horse has the smallest stomach compared to its body size of any domestic animal. This is why horses are constantly eating small amounts of food. They have no place to store a huge meal! The stomach stores food, continues digestion, and sends broken-down food to the small intestine.

BITS & BOBS

Horses have a third eyelid that lies on the inside of the eye **and closes diagonally over it.**

JJS Summer Breeze, a mare from Kansas, U.S.A., had the **LONGEST HORSE TAIL EVER RECORDED,** measuring **12 feet 6 inches (381 cm) long.**

A **horse's hoof** is not a **foot but a** toenail.

A horse's **teeth** occupy more space in its head than its **brain** does.

AN AVERAGE ADULT HORSE'S **HEART WEIGHS 10 POUNDS** (4.5 KG), WHICH **IS 16 TIMES HEAVIER** THAN AN ADULT HUMAN HEART.

Part of a horse's hoof is a **triangular-shaped area called the "frog,"** which helps push **blood up** each leg.

A horse's coat is referred to as **"hair"** not as **"fur."**

SOME **HORSES CAN GROW A MUSTACHE.**

A horse can only chew on one side of its mouth at a time.

HORSES HAVE DIFFERENT TYPES OF COATS FOR DIFFERENT SEASONS:
A LIGHT SUMMER COAT, A SHORT WINTER COAT, AND A LONG WINTER COAT.

Horses with **PINK SKIN** can get sunburns.

An average horse can run **20 to 30 miles an hour** (32 to 48 km/h). The fastest Thoroughbred racehorses can run **44 miles an hour** (71 km/h). But the fastest sprint ever recorded was by a Quarter Horse that clocked in at **55 miles an hour** (88.5 km/h).

The **heart of a racehorse** can pump up to 80 gallons (303 L) of blood per minute.

HORSES CAN SLEEP STANDING UP.

Horses can't breathe through their mouths. They only breathe through their nostrils.

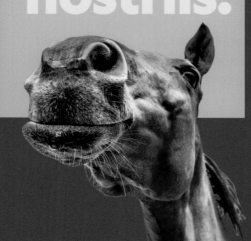

AN AVERAGE **1,000-POUND** (454-KG) **HORSE PRODUCES 56 POUNDS** (25.4 KG) OF **MANURE** EACH DAY.

Horses drink five to **10 gallons** (19 to 38 L) of **water** a day.

Horses can produce at least **10 GALLONS (38 L) OF SALIVA** a day.

THE FLYING HORSE

HORSES HAVE LONG BEEN USED TO TRANSPORT HUMANS.

But, as the role of horses in our society has shifted, humans have had to learn how to transport their horses instead. When horses travel overseas, it can get complicated.

TICKETS PLEASE!

Before a horse can travel internationally, it needs a medical exam. If it is healthy enough to fly, the veterinarian issues a health certificate, which the horse owner brings with the horse's passport. That's right, horses need passports, just like you! The passport includes the horse's name, height, breed, and passport number. It also includes a diagram of the horse and its medical history.

The horse also needs a plane ticket. Just like humans, horses can have different kinds of tickets: economy class (a little squished), business class (a bit more room), and first class (lots of comfy space). With its hay packed and its paperwork in its satchel, the horse is ready to head to the airport.

ALL ABOARD

Horses cannot fly to international locations from every airport. In fact, most countries only have a few "horse-ready" airports. These airports have special "terminals" for horse travelers.

Unlike human passengers who enter a plane and then find their seat, horses are loaded into their "seats" outside the plane. The movable air stalls, or pallets, are then raised by giant lifts and pushed onto the airplane.

In addition to the horse passengers, these flights typically include at least one veterinarian and a number of "flying grooms" who care for the horses. While there is no in-flight entertainment, there is a food and beverage service. The grooms feed the horses hay and water throughout the flight.

HORSES OFTEN RECEIVE CARROTS AT TAKEOFF AND LANDING BECAUSE THE CHEWING HELPS THEIR EARS ADJUST TO PRESSURE CHANGES.

BEFORE AIR TRAVEL BECAME COMMON, HORSES TRAVELED INTERNATIONALLY BY BOAT. SOME OF THEM GOT SEASICK!

PONY PUNS

Q Why did the man stand behind the horse?

A He thought he would get a kick out of it.

Q What do horses see before they hear thunder?

A Lightning colts.

Q What do horses play for fun?

A Stable tennis.

KNOCK, KNOCK.

Who's there?
Toledo.
Toledo who?
Toledo a horse to water is easy. To make him drink is not.

RIDDLE ME THIS ...

Q A horse is tied to a 15-foot (5-m) rope. A bale of hay sits 25 feet (8 m) from the horse. The horse is still able to eat the hay. How is this possible?

A The rope is only tied to the horse.

Q What do young horses wrap their food in?

A Aluminum foal.

Q What's black and white and eats like a horse?

A A zebra.

HAND MEASURING

When your doctor wants to see how tall you are, she measures from the floor you are standing on to the top of your head. She writes down your height in inches (or cm).

A horse is measured from the ground to its withers, which is the area between its shoulder blades. A horse's height is given in hands. But you can't just measure using your own hands. One "hand" is equal to four inches (10.16 cm).

STEP 1:

Stand just behind the horse's front leg.

STEP 2:

Using your tape measure (or length of string), measure from the ground immediately behind the horse's front hoof to the top of its back.

STEP 3:

If you used a string to measure, now measure the length of string that went from the ground to the top of the horse's back.

YOU WILL NEED:

A HORSE TO MEASURE, OR ANY PET OR LARGE STUFFED ANIMAL WILL ALSO WORK!

A TAPE MEASURE OR LENGTH OF STRING

A PEN OR PENCIL AND PAPER TO RECORD YOUR FINDINGS

A CALCULATOR (OPTIONAL)

STEP 4:

One hand is equal to four inches. If you measured the horse's height in inches, divide the number you measured by four. Now you have its height in units of hh (hands high). For example, a horse that is 56 inches tall would be listed as 14 hh. (One hand is also equal to about 10 centimeters. If you measured the horse's height in centimeters, divide the number you measured by 10.)

DURING THE WARMER MONTHS,

THE AMERICAN BASHKIR'S HAIR

IS EITHER **STRAIGHT** OR **WAVY.**
BUT EACH FALL IT GROWS A

CURLY COAT

TO KEEP WARM.

FOALS ARE BORN WITH CURLY COATS, CURLY HAIR IN THEIR EARS, AND EVEN **CURLY EYELASHES.**

ALL THE PRETTY HORSES

From coat colors to beauty marks, horses are as pretty to look at as they are fun to ride! Can you match each of these horse features with the photo? Look at the bottom of the page for the correct answers.

1

2

3

4

A
A LITTLE BIT OF WHITE AT THE TIP OF THE NOSE

B
A PATCH OF WHITE ON THE FOREHEAD

C
A THIN LINE OF WHITE FROM FOREHEAD TO NOSE

D
A THICK LINE OF WHITE FROM FOREHEAD TO NOSE

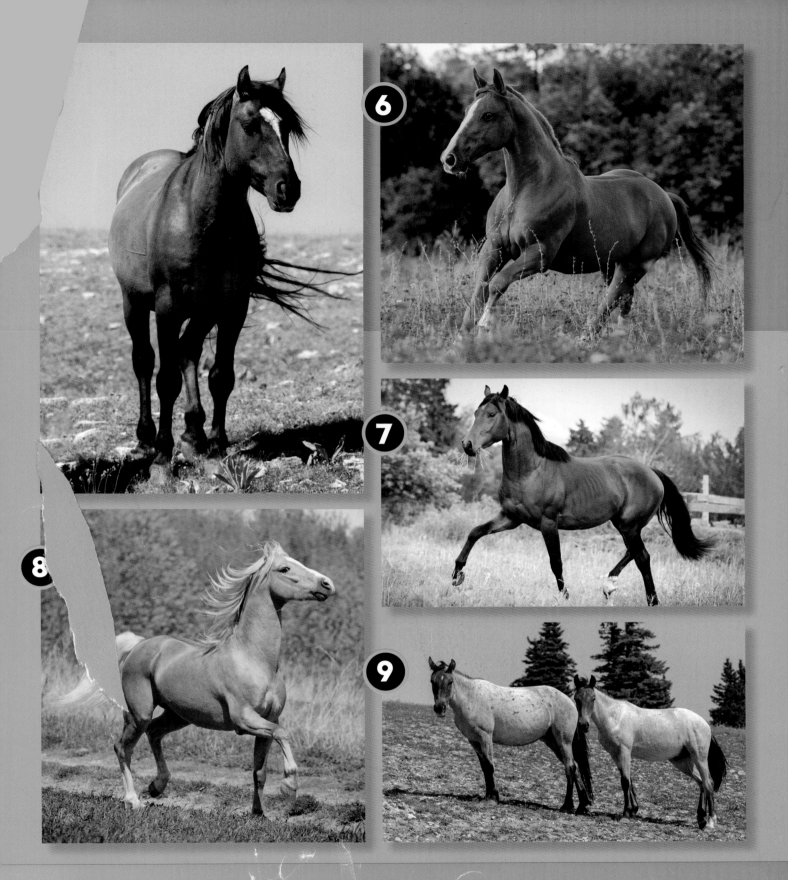

6

7

8

9

E

BROWN BODY,
BLACK MARKINGS

F

BROWN BODY,
RED MARKINGS

G

GRAY OR SILVER BODY,
BLACK MARKINGS

H

EVEN MIX OF CHESTNUT
AND WHITE HAIRS

I

CREAM BODY, WHITE
MANE AND TAIL

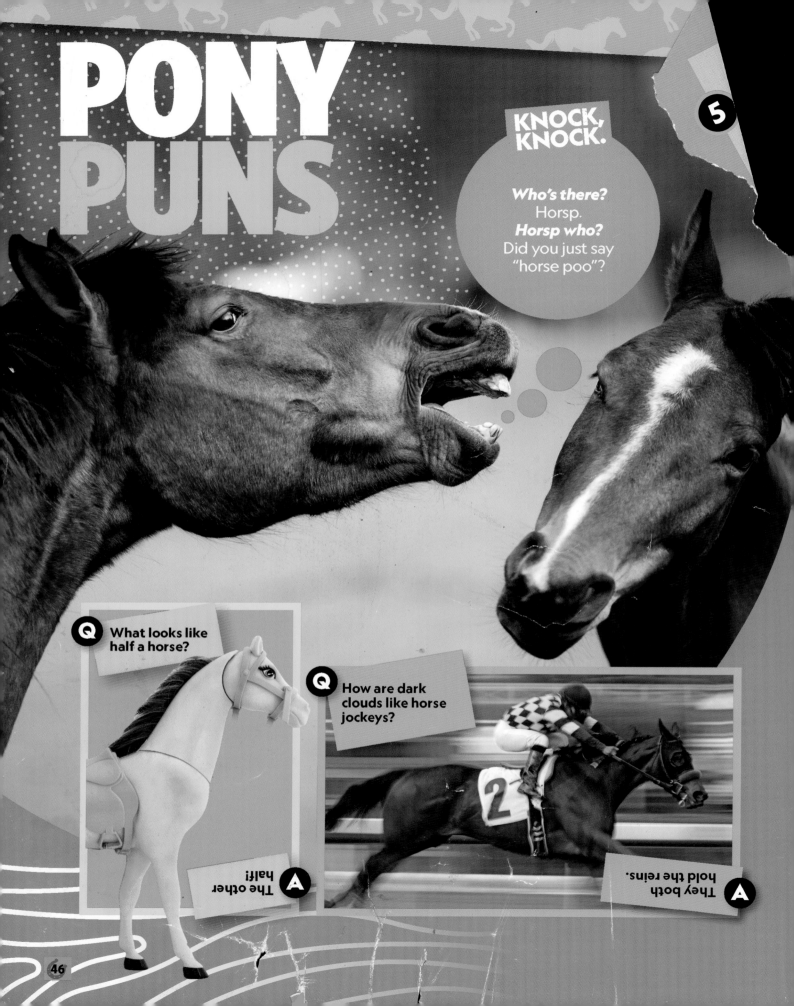

PONY PUNS

KNOCK, KNOCK.

Who's there?
Horsp.
Horsp who?
Did you just say "horse poo"?

Q What looks like half a horse?

A The other half!

Q How are dark clouds like horse jockeys?

A They both hold the reins.

Q Which horse can jump higher than a house?

A All of them. Houses can't jump.

RIDDLE ME THIS ...

Q What's as big as a horse but weighs nothing?

Q What is a vampire's favorite part of a horse race?

A When it's neck and neck.

Q Who were the two most famous horse thieves?

A Bonnie and Clydesdale.

A The horse's shadow.

SUPERSTAR STEEDS

THESE HORSES SET MIND-BOGGLING RECORDS.

FASTEST HORSE ON TWO LEGS

AKHAN

An Akhal-Teke horse named Akhan ran 32.8 feet (10 m) in only 4.19 seconds on just his hind legs. That trampled the previous record of 9.21 seconds.

OLDEST HORSE

OLD BILLY

Horses usually live 25 to 30 years. But the appropriately named Old Billy, born in 1760 in England, lived to the age of 62.

7' 2.5"   6'

TALLEST HORSE

SAMPSON

The tallest horse in history was a Shire named Sampson. Born in 1846 in England, Sampson stood 21 hands plus 2.5 inches tall (7 feet 2.5 inches [2 m 20 cm]).

HIGHEST JUMPER

LASTIC

Lastic, a gray Trakehner gelding, set the British show-jumping high jump record in 1978 by jumping over an obstacle 7 feet 7 inches (2.32 m) high. Lastic could have jumped over Sampson with a few inches to spare!

FABULOUS FASHION

In 1911, Charles Owens invented the first safety helmet. It was made of **cork.**

For three centuries ending in the early 1900s, **CHINESE HORSEBACK RIDERS** wore a type of jacket called a *MAGUA.* A magua tended to be a simple garment, with five disk-shaped buttons down the front, sleeves that were short and wide, and sometimes a square patch on the chest.

In Argentina, Chile, and Uruguay, equestrians wear bombachas, which are wide-legged pants made of cotton.

Beginning over 1,500 years ago, **Japanese men wore** *HAKAMA,* or an ankle-length dress, every day. A special type was worn for horseback-riding. It had a split at the bottom, which made it more like trousers, but it still had a billowy look.

FOR SAFETY, MODERN EQUESTRIANS SOMETIMES WEAR AIR VESTS, WHICH WORK LIKE AN AIR BAG IN A CAR. THEY INFLATE WITH AIR IF THE RIDER FALLS FROM THE SADDLE.

In the **1700s,** European men and women both wore military-influenced jackets with gold or silver braids and ornamental buttons for riding.

Because European women **wore skirts** while riding, they rode **sidesaddle,** with both legs hanging off one side of the horse.

JODHPURS are wide-hipped, tight-ankled riding trousers that originated in Jodhpur, India. They became very popular outside of India in the 1900s, as they allowed for upper leg movement while riding.

In the Middle Eastern country of Jordan, men often wear a **KAFFIYEH,** a cotton scarf wrapped around the head to protect them from sun, sand, and dust while riding.

51

DESIGN YOUR DREAM RIDING HABIT

WHETHER YOU HAVE ALWAYS DREAMED OF WHAT YOU WOULD WEAR IN THE SHOW RING, OR YOU JUST WANT TO PUT TOGETHER AN AWESOME OUTFIT FOR JAUNTS AROUND THE FARM, USE THIS EXERCISE TO CREATE A MINI PATTERN FOR YOUR PERFECT RIDING OUTFIT. DON'T FORGET TO INCLUDE AN IMAGE OF YOUR HORSE SO THAT YOU CAN SEE HOW THE DREAM OUTFIT WORKS WITH YOUR DREAM MOUNT!

Dressage is a sport in which people compete to show mastery of their horses. Competitors are supposed to dress in a way that won't distract from the horse ... and the rider's control of it. This can make it difficult for a competitor to put together a unique outfit. Clothing for dressage hasn't changed much in hundreds of years, but you can use your imagination in this activity!

YOU WILL NEED:

PENCIL

SCISSORS

GLUE

CONSTRUCTION PAPER

COLORED PENCILS OR MARKERS

RHINESTONES, PIPING, EMBROIDERY (OPTIONAL)

STEP 1:

Find your favorite clothing items from your closet and draw them on pieces of colorful construction paper (choose whichever colors you like for your pieces!). Then cut them out.

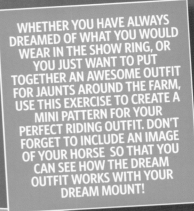

STEP 2:

Glue your cutouts to another piece of construction paper and carefully cut them out again for added structure.

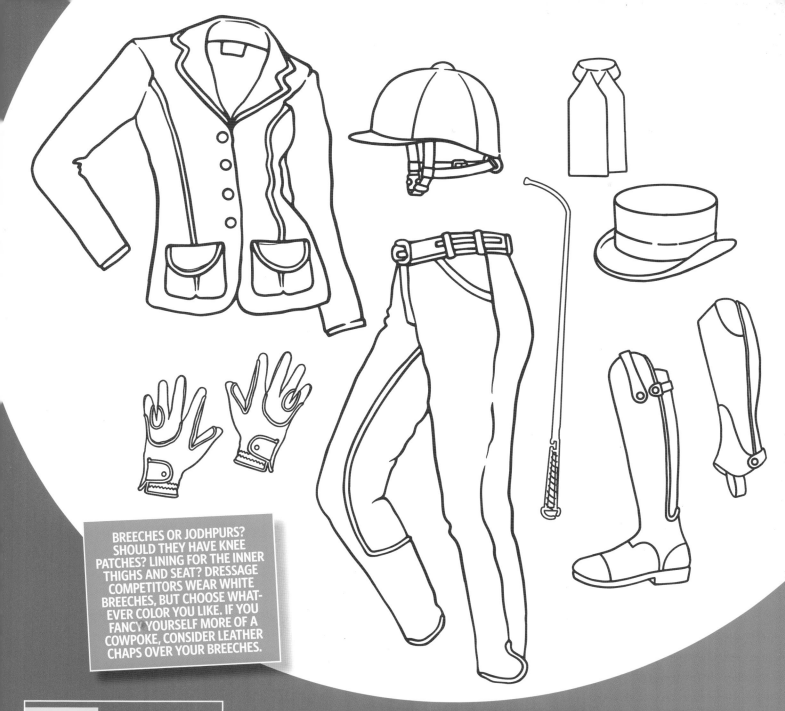

BREECHES OR JODHPURS? SHOULD THEY HAVE KNEE PATCHES? LINING FOR THE INNER THIGHS AND SEAT? DRESSAGE COMPETITORS WEAR WHITE BREECHES, BUT CHOOSE WHAT-EVER COLOR YOU LIKE. IF YOU FANCY YOURSELF MORE OF A COWPOKE, CONSIDER LEATHER CHAPS OVER YOUR BREECHES.

STEP 3:

Decorate your pieces however you like!

STEP 4:

You now have pieces for your dream dressage outfit! Don't forget to add an image of your dream horse!

THINGS TO CONSIDER

How do you want to protect your head? Dressage competitors used to wear top hats, but they now wear helmets with a short peak (brim). Dressage rules require riders to wear something in a muted color (like black, brown, gray, or navy blue). But don't feel like you need to choose from these colors or even just one color. For this activity, be creative. The sky's the limit! Consider putting stripes down the middle or an image of a horse on the side. Decorate with stones or piping or embroidery. Don't like the look of a helmet with a peak? Ditch it. A helmet without a peak is called a skull.

THE
MARWARI HORSE
IS KNOWN FOR
ITS CURVED EARS, WHICH
SLOPE SO FAR THAT
THE TIPS
OFTEN TOUCH EACH OTHER.

THIS HORSE COMES FROM THE MARWAR REGION OF INDIA, PART OF WHICH LIES IN THE THAR DESERT. THE MARWARI HORSE HAS SHOULDER BONES THAT ARE LESS SLANTED THAN THOSE OF OTHER BREEDS. THIS HELPS IT WALK OR TROT ACROSS DEEP DESERT SAND.

HOW HUMANS DOMESTICATED HORSES

DR. WILLIAM TAYLOR, ARCHAEOLOGIST

Archaeologists like me study the way people lived a long time ago. My passion is figuring out when humans started using horses to carry our things and take us from place to place. It can be tricky to find the answer because humans domesticated horses long before we started writing anything down.

DEFINING DOMESTICATION

People often think horses were domesticated when we first began to ride them. But you can tame an animal to be ridden without it being domesticated. For example, you can find old pictures of people riding moose, elk, or zebras.

Archaeologists define a domestic animal as one whose reproduction is human-controlled. That is, humans are directly involved in managing how these animals mate, breed, and reproduce.

A BIG CLUE

Horses evolved in North America, but even though they were hunted by ancient people

EXCAVATING IN MONGOLIA

in this area for centuries, they probably went extinct on that continent 10,000 years ago. Horses were only reintroduced to North America 500 years ago. During more recent times, when we have historic documents to go alongside our archaeological finds, we can see in great detail what happened when people adopted domestic horses into their lives. It changed everything.

Knowing the effect that horse domestication had on people in North America gave us clues about what to look for when we try to find evidence of the earliest domestication of horses in Eurasia. Horse domestication meant people could travel huge distances. And they did, immediately! They started trading goods across continents. They started fighting more wars. Religious ceremonies changed. After chariots were invented—boom!—horses were all across Europe and Asia within a couple hundred years. Horses are so transformative that it makes the evidence easier to find.

WILLIAM TAYLOR
EXAMINES ROCK ART
OF A HORSE AND RIDER AT
PICTURE CANYON IN SOUTHERN
COLORADO, U.S.A., LIKELY MADE
BY THE COMANCHE PEOPLE—
ONE OF THE GREAT HORSE
CULTURES OF WESTERN
NORTH AMERICA.

EQUINE ATHLETES

🏵 BEST DANCER

VALEGRO

Valegro, a dark bay-colored Dutch Warmblood, competed in dressage, an event in which horses perform a series of movements set to music. Valegro, known to his friends as Blueberry, won gold medals at the World Cup Finals, the World Equestrian Games, the European Dressage Championships, and the 2012 and 2016 Olympics.

🏵 FIRST EQUINE ATHLETES

TETHRIPPON COMPETITORS

In 680 B.C., chariot racing became an Olympic event in Greece. The race, called the tethrippon, featured chariots pulled by four horses. The competing chariots raced 10 or 12 times around the hippodrome, which was a flat, open field.

BIGGEST HEART

SECRETARIAT

Secretariat was an American Thoroughbred that won the Triple Crown in 1973. Earning a Triple Crown means that in one season he won three major races: the Kentucky Derby, the Preakness Stakes, and the Belmont Stakes. He set, and still holds, the fastest time record in all three races. When Secretariat died, veterinarians estimated that his heart weighed 21 pounds (9.5 kg), roughly twice the size of his competitors.

HIGHEST JUMPER

STROLLER

Stroller, a bay-colored Thoroughbred/Connemara mix, was the first pony to compete at the Olympics in show jumping. He won the silver medal in 1968. At the ripe old age of 20, Stroller also became the first pony to win the Hamburg Derby.

A HELPING HOOF

Horses help plants! When a horse eats seeds in one place and poops them out in another, the plants are introduced to new areas.

Police use horses and their efficient locomotion and elevated height for **search and rescue missions.**

HORSES EAT ALL DAY, WHICH RESULTS IN A LOT OF HORSE POOP. HORSE POOP IS A **NATURAL FERTILIZER.** USING IT FOR THAT PURPOSE CAN CUT DOWN ON THE AMOUNT OF HUMAN-MADE FERTILIZERS THAT RESULT IN AIR AND WATER POLLUTION.

Riding a **horse** is great exercise that helps your body stay healthy.

LIKE OTHER PETS, HORSES PROVIDE LOVE AND COMPANIONSHIP. THEY ARE KNOWN TO IMPROVE PEOPLE'S MENTAL HEALTH.

The **U.S. Space Force** recruited a mustang named Ghost to patrol Vandenburg Air Force Base, a 100,000-acre (40,469-ha) parcel of land in Southern California. Ghost boldly goes to parts of the base that cars cannot. The military currently has no plans to send Ghost into space.

Like yoga or Pilates, riding a horse can **improve your core strength.** A strong core helps a rider stay centered on the saddle.

HORSEBACK RIDING CAN ALSO REDUCE BLOOD PRESSURE, WHICH IN TURN REDUCES THE RISK OF HEART DISEASE.

BLOW PAINT A PINTO

Do you like painting? Then this activity will hit the spot for you. A pinto horse is any breed of horse that has a dark coat color with white markings on it. Like snowflakes, no two pinto horses have the same exact appearance. In this activity, you will make your own unique pinto horse markings.

STEP 1:

Pick your base color. The three main base colors for a pinto are bay (black and red hairs), black (only black hairs), and chestnut (only red hairs).

WARNING: ASK AN ADULT TO HELP YOU CHOOSE SAFE PAINT AND TO SUPERVISE THE PAINTING.

STEP 2:

Choose a sheet of cardboard, card stock, or white paper. Use markers to draw and color in a horse with the base color you want.

STEP 3:

Cut your straw to half the length. This will make it easier to direct the paint.

YOU WILL NEED:

CARDBOARD, CARD STOCK, OR WHITE PAPER
COLORED MARKERS
PLASTIC STRAW
WHITE NONTOXIC PAINT
SMALL, DISPOSABLE CUP
SCISSORS

STEP 4:

Ask an adult to poke a hole in the shortened straw about halfway up, so that you can't accidentally slurp the paint.

STEP 5:

Pour some white paint into a small, disposable cup. If the paint is thick, add water until it is runny.

STEP 6:

Place your straw in the paint, and then place your thumb over the straw. This will trap some paint in the straw. Keeping your thumb on the straw, move it over your horse.

STEP 7:

Release your thumb from the end of the straw to allow the paint to splatter onto your horse.

STEP 8:

Place your mouth over the clean end of your straw. Gently blow the paint to create a pattern on your horse. Experiment with how hard to blow, or see how it works with different-size straws.

NEED MORE OF A CHALLENGE? SEE IF YOU CAN RE-CREATE THE COMMON FACE MARKINGS IN THE BOXES AT RIGHT.

STAR   STRIPE   BLAZE   SNIPE   BALD FACE

IF YOUR PINTO HORSE IS BLACK WITH WHITE SPOTS, IT IS CALLED PIEBALD. IF YOU CHOSE ANY OTHER BASE COLOR, YOUR HORSE IS CALLED SKEWBALD.

YOU CAN USE THIS DRAWING TO TRACE YOUR HORSE. OR TRY DRAWING YOUR OWN!

HORSING AROUND WITH COMPANION GOATS

HORSES ARE HERD ANIMALS. They like to have friends around. When a horse is lonely, it may get nervous. It may pace around its stall or rock from side to side. It may even stop eating. Even if its owner wants to get a horse a pasture pal, a second horse is expensive! Thankfully, horses and goats go together like peas and carrots.

BARN BUDDIES

Goats are also herd animals, so they want friends just like horses do. Because they are much smaller than horses, they cost less to keep and do not require as much space. If the horse needs to travel, the goat can easily tag along—much easier than bringing along a second horse. Both animals eat hay, but, if you allow them to graze, a goat will eat the weeds and leave the grass for the horse. Another plus: Goats and horses do not get each other sick. This means that illnesses that affect one cannot be passed to the other.

CAREFUL WHAT YOU WISH FOR

On the other hand, goats can cause problems. They are escape artists, so they may be able to get around (or climb over) fences that would contain a horse. If you feed either animal store-bought feed, you have to be careful that the other cannot reach it. Goat feed can poison a horse and vice versa. And sometimes goats can mistake a horse's tail for a delicious snack. Yikes!

Finally, the horse and goat may not become fast friends. Horse owners should introduce the animals slowly to let them get used to each other. They should be separated by a fence for a few days so they can see and smell one another. And hopefully, before long, they will be neighing and bleating around the pasture together.

THE PHRASE "GOT YOUR GOAT" MEANS THAT SOMETHING ANNOYED YOU. ACCORDING TO LEGEND, IT COMES FROM THE ONE-TIME PRACTICE OF JOCKEYS STEALING AN OPPONENT'S GOAT. WITHOUT A GOAT BUDDY BY ITS SIDE, THE HORSE MIGHT PERFORM POORLY IN A RACE.

GOATS LIKE TO CLIMB. IT IS NOT UNCOMMON FOR A COMPANION GOAT TO CLIMB ONTO THE BACK OF ITS HORSE ... AND RIDE AROUND THE PASTURE.

TRIVIA TROT

HAVE YOU PICKED UP ANY EQUINE TRIVIA ALONG THIS OLD DUSTY TRAIL? YOU'RE ABOUT TO FIND OUT! WRITE YOUR ANSWERS ON A SEPARATE PIECE OF PAPER AND THEN CHECK THE ANSWER KEY BELOW. IF YOU CAN'T FIGURE OUT AN ANSWER, LOOK BACK THROUGH THE FIRST HALF OF THE BOOK.

1 Shetland ponies once worked in ___ .

   a. coal mines

   b. salt mines

   c. gold mines

   d. Minecraft

2 Most foals stand within ___ .

a. one month after birth

b. one week after birth

c. one hour after birth

d. one day after birth

3 True or False?

Horses burp when they eat radishes.

4 A horse's coat is referred to as ___ .

   a. fur

   b. hair

   c. wool

   d. a jacket

5 To measure a horse's height, you measure from the ground to the top of its ___ .

   a. head

   b. tail

   c. kneecap

   d. shoulder blades

6 The oldest horse in history lived until it was in its ___ .

   a. 40s

   b. 50s

   c. 60s

   d. 70s

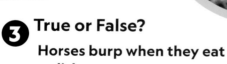

7 The Marwari horse is known for its ears. What is so special about them?

  a. They can hear a pin drop from a mile away.

  b. They can rotate 180 degrees.

  c. They are curved so far that the tips almost touch.

  d. They point at what the horse is looking at.

8 Valegro, the famous dressage horse, was nicknamed ___ .

  a. Blueberry

  b. Blackberry

  c. Strawberry

  d. Ted

9 A black horse with white spots is called ___ .

  a. cakebald

  b. piebald

  c. browniebald

  d. a zebra

10 Which of the following animals does NOT share a common ancestor with the horse?

  a. rhinoceros

  b. zebra

  c. Przewalski's horse

  d. elephant

11 Which of the following does a horse NOT need in order to fly to another country?

  a. passport

  b. health certificate

  c. driver's license

  d. plane ticket

12 True or False?

An elephant has larger eyes than a horse.

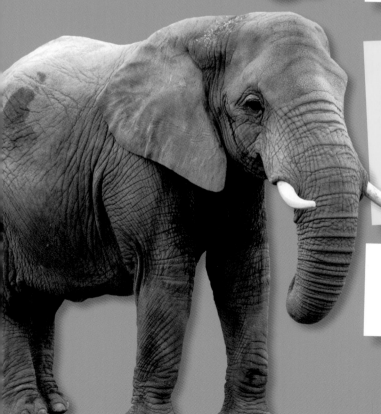

ANSWERS: 1. a; 2. c; 3. False; 4. b; 5. d; 6. c; 7. c; 8. a; 9. b; 10. d; 11. c; 12. False

PONY PUNS

KNOCK, KNOCK.

Who's there?
Neigh-neigh.
Neigh-neigh who?
Make up your mind!
Are you a horse
or an owl?

Q Why did the
woman name
her horse Mayo?

A Because Mayo
neighs.

Q Why should you always
be polite to a jockey
who likes to jump?

A So he doesn't
take a fence.

Q What street do horses live on?

A Mane Street.

Q What do you call a horse that is not wearing a saddle?

A Neigh-ked.

RIDDLE ME THIS ...

Q A woman rode up a hill on Friday. The next day she rode back on Friday, too. How is this possible?

A The horse is named Friday.

Q Why did the horse cross the road?

A Because someone shouted "Hay!"

FREE-ROAMING HOROSES

SYLVIA JOHNSON, FILM DIRECTOR

I like to make documentaries (nonfiction movies) about nature and what people need to do to protect it. I made the movie *Roaming Wild* about mustangs after a friend took me to see how the U.S. government uses helicopters to round up horses before sending them off to live in pens. They do this to reduce the population of wild horses on public lands and to remove them from areas where ranchers allow their animals (like cows and sheep) to forage. It was incredible to see these wild animals run across the beautiful landscape, but it was horrifying to see them run away from the helicopter in abject terror.

NOT ENOUGH LAND

The federal government manages a lot of land in the United States. The amount of life that this land can healthily sustain is limited. If much of the land is used to graze cattle, for example, there is less land for horses. So it is a constant effort to find a balance. The only way to arrive at a solution that is humane for the horses is to also understand the needs of the people who rely on the land for food and income.

TOO MANY HORSES?

Around 86,000 mustangs live on public land. That number does not include the 55,000 mustangs that the government has already removed. The government tries to find homes for these horses, but only a very small percentage of the horses who are removed are adopted. Most live out their lives in holding facilities.

In my movie, we suggest that one way to manage the horse population is for the government to treat the mustangs with drugs that prevent the horses from having babies. After the movie came out, the government started giving one fertility control drug, PZP, to a couple of small herds throughout the West. But the government still relies more on removal to reduce the number of mustangs.

HORSE HUMOR

KNOCK, KNOCK.

Who's there?
Anita
Anita who?
I need a good laugh!

Q Why was the racehorse nicknamed "Bad News"?

News Today
BAD NEWS!!

A Everyone knows that bad news travels fast.

Q What do you call the horse who lives next door?

A A neigh-bor.

TONGUE TWISTER

SAY THIS FAST THREE TIMES:

The racehorse ran rings around the Roman ruins.

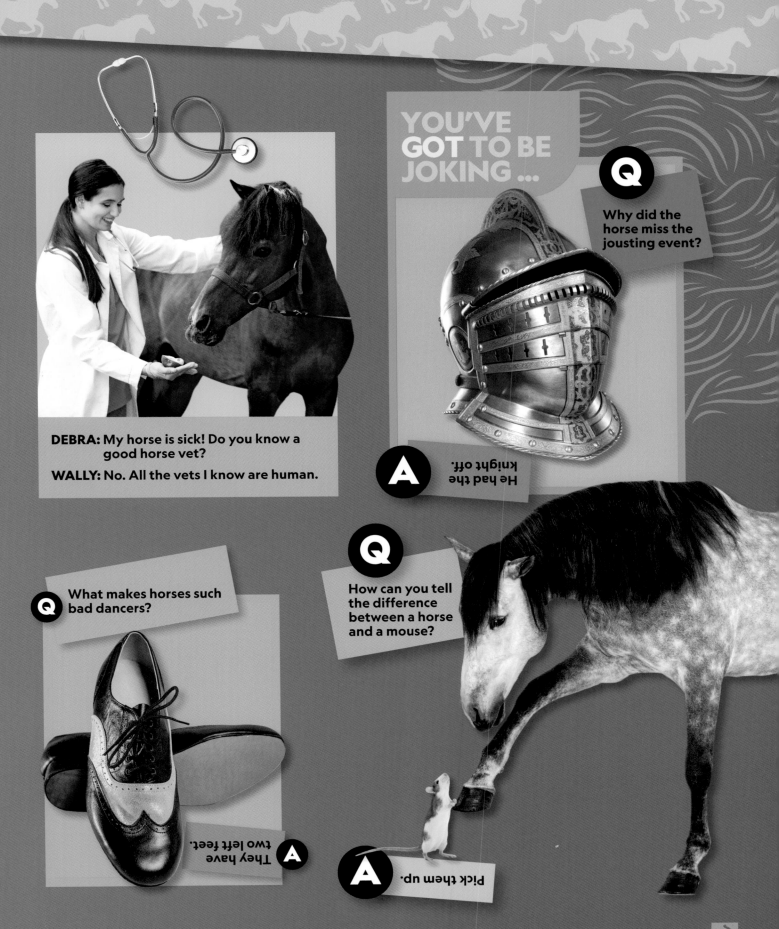

YOU'VE GOT TO BE JOKING ...

DEBRA: My horse is sick! Do you know a good horse vet?

WALLY: No. All the vets I know are human.

Q Why did the horse miss the jousting event?

A He had the knight off.

Q What makes horses such bad dancers?

A They have two left feet.

Q How can you tell the difference between a horse and a mouse?

A Pick them up.

HORSE GAITS

Just as humans can walk, jog, skip, or run, horses can move in many different ways, or gaits. Each gait moves the horse at a different speed. Giddyup!

TROT
When a horse trots, its left front and right hind strike the ground at the same time, followed by its right front and left hind. That is, one diagonal pair of hooves strikes the ground and then the other diagonal pair follows. The trot also includes a moment of suspension, when all four hooves are off the ground at the same time. The average speed of a trot is 7 to 10 miles an hour (11 to 16 km/h).

3.5 to 4 mph
(5 to 6 km/h)

WALK
When a horse walks, each of its hooves strikes the ground one after the other: right front, left hind, left front, right hind. The average speed of a walk is 3.5 to 4 miles an hour (5 to 6 km/h).

7 to 10 mph
(11 to 16 km/h)

CANTER
When a horse canters with its right hoof leading, its left hind foot strikes first, followed by its right hind and left front feet striking at the same time, followed by its right front foot. There is again a moment of suspension. The average speed of a canter is 6 to 17 miles an hour (9 to 27 km/h).

10 to 17 mph
(16 to 27 km/h)

25 to 40 mph
(40 to 64 km/h)

GALLOP
When a horse gallops, each of its hooves strikes the ground one after the other—the same as when it walks. But its hooves strike in a different order: right hind, left hind, right front, left front, and there is a moment of suspension. The average speed of a gallop is 25 to 40 miles an hour (40 to 64 km/h).

MYTHICAL HORSES

In Norse mythology, the god Odin rode an **EIGHT-LEGGED HORSE CALLED SLEIPNIR** that could carry its rider to each of the nine realms, including the **LAND OF THE DEAD.**

In Hindu folklore, **UCHCHAIHSHRAVAS** is a white, winged horse with **SEVEN HEADS.** It was known as the king of the horses.

The **UNICORN,** depicted as a horse with a single spiral horn on its forehead, was said to **HEAL** anyone who drank from its **HORN.**

In medieval legends, a **HIPPOGRIFF** was a creature with the body of a horse and the head, wings, and talons of a **GRIFFIN.** It was typically ridden by either a knight or a sorcerer.

IN GREEK MYTHOLOGY, THE **HIPPOCAMPUS** WAS A HORSE WITH THE TAIL OF A FISH THAT PULLED THE CHARIOT OF **POSEIDON,** THE SEA GOD.

In Scottish folklore, **KELPIES** were spirits who haunted lakes or rivers. Often depicted as **BLACK HORSES,** kelpies could change into human form.

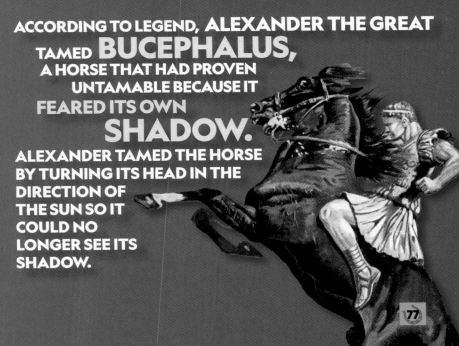

ACCORDING TO LEGEND, **ALEXANDER THE GREAT** TAMED **BUCEPHALUS,** A HORSE THAT HAD PROVEN UNTAMABLE BECAUSE IT **FEARED ITS OWN SHADOW.** ALEXANDER TAMED THE HORSE BY TURNING ITS HEAD IN THE DIRECTION OF THE SUN SO IT COULD NO LONGER SEE ITS SHADOW.

EQUINE NUTRITION

HOW AN EVOLVING WORK/LIFE BALANCE CHANGED HORSES' DIETS

ALL-NATURAL DIET

The earliest known ancestor of the modern horse was a creature called Eohippus that lived 50 million years ago. It was the size of a dog, lived in the forest, and ate leaves and fruit. It was nothing like the horses we are familiar with today.

Over the next 45 million years, the forests of North America became grass-covered plains. The modern horse came into existence (and survived) because it developed an efficient method of getting nutrition from grass. It grew very large. Its longer limbs allowed it to run quickly from predators and to travel long distances in search of grass.

HORSE MEETS HUMAN

Some 6,000 years ago, humans domesticated horses. Rather than foraging for grass about 15 hours per day, horses now worked for humans. Since they burned a lot of energy plowing our fields, horses needed even more food than they did when they roamed the prairie. But they had no time to eat. They were too busy working! To solve this problem, humans fed horses dried grass called hay. Dried grass provides more energy per mouthful than live grass. If the horse worked really hard, humans would feed it oats or corn in addition to hay. Since horses have small stomachs, humans still fed them many small meals each day, just as horses would eat in the wild.

HUMAN MEETS TRACTOR

Just over 100 years ago, humans started replacing horses with machines. Today, people mostly keep horses for recreation and companionship. But a horse's current diet is often similar to what they ate when they were working. And that creates all sorts of problems for them. Humans are still experimenting with feeding horses the right things in the right way. Since horses do not do well eating two large meals a day, humans can provide food for them with a slow feeder, which lets out multiple small portions throughout the day. While nothing can replace some 15 hours of grazing, we are doing our best to mimic the way horses were designed to eat.

BALANCING ACT

Horse blood contains water and salt in a very precise balance. When the horse urinates, the amount of water in its blood goes down, but the amount of salt stays the same. Since its blood is now too salty, the horse's brain tells it to drink some water to restore the water-salt balance.

Horse sweat also contains water and salt. In fact, it contains water and salt in roughly the same balance as what is in the horse's blood. But when a horse sweats, it loses both water and salt. Since the balance of salt to water in its blood hasn't changed, its brain doesn't think it is thirsty ... even though it is. This is why you can lead a domesticated horse to water, but you can't make it drink. The horse doesn't realize it needs water!

HORSE SCRAMBLE

It looks like someone turned over the horse cart! The letters in these horse names have been jumbled. Unscramble the letters in each name to identify the type of horse pictured. Write your answers on a separate sheet of paper. Then compare them to the answer key at the bottom of the page. On your mark. Get set. Go!

1 NAORGM

2 MECIRANA AQTURRE HRESO

3 RWARIMA

4 DOHBHREOTRUG

5 YSEALCELDD

6 PPSAAOALO

7 NAUYAKTI

8 AAIABNR

BRAIDING A HORSE'S MANE CAN HELP KEEP IT **HEALTHY** BY PREVENTING ITS HAIR FROM BREAKING, KEEPING IT OUT OF THE **HORSE'S EYES,** AND KEEPING IT FREE FROM DIRT.

HORSE MANES CAN GROW UP TO **THREE TIMES FASTER** THAN HUMAN HAIR CAN.

PONY PUNS

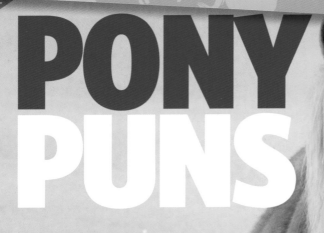

Q What do you call a horse at the North Pole?

A Lost.

Q Why was the horse so unhappy?

A He was saddled with a lot of problems.

Q Why did the horse go over the mountain?

A He couldn't go under it.

Q What does a horse say when she finishes eating?

A That's the last straw.

Q How is a horse like a banana?

A They're both bright yellow ... except for the horse.

Q What do you call a horse that likes to run along the surf?

A A seahorse.

RIDDLE ME THIS ...

Q How do you get your horse to go exactly the same speed as a train?

A You let him ride on it.

HORSE COMMUNICATION

HORSES CAN'T SPEAK, BUT THEY CAN TELL US A LOT WITH THEIR BODY LANGUAGE.

By paying attention to the position of their ears and the swishing of their tails, humans can understand much of what a horse is trying to say.

FEARFUL

As a prey animal, a horse can easily get scared. When a horse is scared, it holds its head up high and the muscles in its neck tense. It wants to be ready to bolt from danger. Its ears will either point at the source of its fear or rotate back and forth listening for it. Its eyes will get wide and look for the best escape route. It may also flare its nostrils and tuck its tail tightly against its hindquarters.

ANGRY

When a horse is angry, it will pin its ears against its head, and it may curl its lip or show its teeth. It may lower its head and "snake" it from side to side. If it starts pawing the ground forcefully, it may be getting ready to charge. If it starts swinging its back legs around, it may be getting ready to kick.

CALM

When a horse is not looking for a treat or thinking about whether to run from an object in the distance, it may relax. Its eyes will partially close. Its lower lip may droop. Its head will drop, forming a straight line from its back to its neck to its head. Its ears will point out to the sides.

HORSES CAN MAKE 17 DIFFERENT FACIAL EXPRESSIONS TO COMMUNICATE. THAT IS FOUR MORE THAN CHIMPANZEES AND ONLY 10 FEWER THAN HUMANS.

WHEN HORSES CURL THEIR TOP LIP UP, IT CAN LOOK AS IF THEY ARE SMILING. BUT THIS BEHAVIOR, CALLED THE FLEHMEN RESPONSE, ALLOWS THE HORSE TO PICK UP SCENTS IN THE AIR.

LIFE IN THE HERD

A **HERD** of wild horses traveling together is called a **HAREM** or band.

A **DOMINANT** horse expects a submissive horse to move out of its way and can become **AGGRESSIVE** when this doesn't happen.

THE **STALLION** IS THE DOMINANT MEMBER OF THE GROUP, OR **ALPHA,** BUT THE BAND USUALLY FOLLOWS THE DIRECTION OF THE ADULT FEMALE HORSES, OR **MARES.**

Male and female HORSE PAIRS can stay together for MANY YEARS.

FOALS

must quickly learn what the different sounds and behaviors of the adult horses mean. If an adult horse tightens its muscles or widens its pupils or pins its ears back, the foal learns to **GET READY TO RUN.**

WHILE OTHER WILD, **HOOFED MAMMALS** ROAM IN LARGER GROUPS, ONLY THREE TO 10 HORSES MAKE UP A **BAND.**

THE STALLION OFTEN TRAVELS AT THE **BACK** OF THE HERD TO MAKE SURE THE GROUP IS **SAFE.**

If a **NEW HORSE** joins the herd, play fighting or real fighting often occurs to see where that horse fits into the **PECKING ORDER.**

To get rid of **FLIES,** horses will stand head-to-tail in a line to **HELP EACH OTHER** swat away the bugs.

Horses play fight by **NIPPING** at each other's **KNEES AND FACES.** If one horse becomes a **BULLY,** another horse will usually **TRY TO STOP IT.**

Horses in a herd **GROOM** each other to show **AFFECTION.**

When horses greet other members of their group, they make

HAPPY NICKERING SOUNDS.

HORSES **TRUST** OTHERS IN THEIR GROUP. IF ONE HORSE RUNS AWAY FROM SOMETHING, THE OTHERS **FOLLOW** FIRST AND ASK QUESTIONS LATER.

HORSE MATCHING

Think you already know everything about horses? See if you can match each of the following words with its correct definition. Write your answers (numbered 1 through 20) on a separate piece of paper. Then compare them to the answer key at the bottom of the page.

1 COLT	2 REIN	3 FOAL	4 TACK
5 STIRRUP	6 CINCH	7 GALLOP	8 DAM
9 MARE	10 CANTLE	11 BUCK	12 BRIDLE
13 CANTER	14 FILLY	15 TROT	16 CRUPPER
17 BRONCO	18 BIT	19 BREASTPLATE	20 STALLION

A

The strap that goes around the horse's midsection to hold the saddle on

B

A female horse usually under four years old

C

The fastest of the equine gaits

D

The piece of tack that goes on the horse's head to control the horse

E

A horse that works in the rodeo, bucking off cowboys

F

A female horse more than four years old

G

The metal part of the bridle that goes in the horse's mouth

H

A male horse over four years of age that can still produce offspring

I

A male horse usually under four years old

J

The three-beat gait that is faster than a trot but slower than a gallop

K

A piece of leather under the horse's tail that keeps the saddle from sliding forward

L

A long, narrow strap attached to a horse's bit, typically used as a pair to guide or check a horse

M

A mother horse

N

A leather piece of tack that goes across the horse's chest to keep the saddle in place

O

The back part of the saddle seat

P

A device attached to each side of the saddle that supports the rider's feet

Q

When a horse lands on its front left and rear right legs, then lands on its front right and rear left legs

R

A young horse, either male or female

S

When a horse kicks its hind legs into the air while its front legs remain on the ground

T

The equipment worn by horses to carry a rider, such as saddles, stirrups, and reins

ANSWERS: 1. I; 2. L; 3. R; 4. T; 5. P; 6. A; 7. C; 8. M; 9. F; 10. O; 11. S; 12. D; 13. J; 14. B; 15. Q; 16. K; 17. E; 18. G; 19. N; 20. H

WHAT HORSE-RELATED JOB IS
RIGHT FOR YOU?

If you can't get enough of horses, maybe you would like a career in the horse world. But what horse-related job is right for you? To find out, answer these questions. Pick the answer that best matches your feelings but choose only one answer for each question. Write down the letters of your answers on a piece of paper. And remember, there are no right or wrong answers.

IF THESE DESCRIPTIONS DON'T FIT YOU, THAT'S OK. THIS QUIZ IS JUST FOR FUN!

1. What is your favorite article of clothing?

a. my white coat

b. I like to wear uniforms.

c. anything, as long as it is color coordinated and in season

d. shoes

e. My horse likes me the same no matter what I wear.

2. Sweet! You have two hours free this afternoon. How do you spend them?

a. watching a nature documentary

b. hiking a nearby trail

c. I never have an hour free.

d. kicking a soccer ball around with friends

e. drawing pictures of ponies

3. You are planning a trip to New York City. What is your first stop?

a. the Bronx Zoo

b. Central Park

c. a Broadway musical

d. a walking tour

e. say hello to a police horse

4. What is your favorite holiday?

a. Christmas

b. Independence Day

c. Thanksgiving

d. Halloween

e. Valentine's Day

5. It's your last day visiting a new city. Which museum do you visit?

a. the science museum

b. the museum of natural history

c. the art museum

d. the shoe museum

e. the museum of saddles and stirrups

6. **If your family went for a hike, your favorite part would be __ .**

    a. seeing wild animals

    b. everything

    c. nothing

    d. just walking around outside

    e. spotting clouds that look like horses

7. **How do you like to spend your summer vacation?**

    a. volunteering at the local zoo

    b. at an outdoor camp

    c. checking out a different camp every week

    d. taking science classes

    e. coaching younger kids

8. **Time to pick a new hobby! Which do you choose?**

    a. completing puzzles

    b. camping

    c. stamp collecting

    d. woodworking

    e. gardening

CHECK YOUR SCORE. First, add up how many of each letter you have chosen. Then read the results below. If you have a tie score, read the results for both letters:

Three or more a's: You would make an excellent veterinarian!

Veterinarians are the doctors of the animal world. You need to study in college for about four years and then study in a veterinary medical school for another four years. Participating in your local 4-H organization or volunteering at a zoo would also be a plus.

Three or more b's: Consider life as a park ranger.

Rangers often rely on horses to transport them because horses do less harm to the park than a car would. Horses can also get to remote areas more easily. To become a park ranger, you will need to study biology or forestry or earth sciences. You may also want to get some experience working at a museum or your local park.

Three of more c's: You would make a great show manager.

Horses compete in all kinds of events, which don't plan themselves! In addition to gaining some experience with horses and competitions, you should study business and management with some equine studies rolled in.

Three or more d's: Why not try your hand at being a farrier?

You would make sure horses' hooves are trimmed and that their shoes fit correctly. You may also fit injured horses with therapeutic horseshoes. You can start at an accredited farrier school or pick up the basics from an experienced farrier.

Three or more e's (or not three or more of anything): You love horses! Why not become a horse trainer?

You can help horses with behavioral issues or teach them how to carry a rider. You may need to get a degree in equine science, but you mostly just need experience with horses.

MINIATURE THERAPY
HORSE TRAINING

DEBBIE GARCIA-BENGOCHEA, MINIATURE THERAPY HORSE TRAINER

My husband and I started the Gentle Carousel Miniature Therapy Horses charity 25 years ago. At the time, no one else was using miniature horses as therapy horses. There were a lot of therapeutic riding programs, but for those you need to be able to take the patient to the horse. We wanted to take the horse to the patient. Our horses are small enough to move around hospital rooms. Our horses interact with 25,000 people each year, comforting hospital patients and survivors of natural disasters. They have participated in ballet performances, visited baby pandas, roamed the halls of Congress, and received standing ovations at concerts. *Time* magazine named our horse, Magic, one of history's 10 most heroic animals.

WELL TRAINED

The horses train for two years. Horses are prey animals, so they think very differently from us. Imagine how scary it is to get into an elevator. The floor moves! We have arrangements with some local facilities that allow us to use their elevators to train the horses.

The horses also learn to be house-trained. If a horse is visiting a patient in the hospital, she knows to tap her front hoof once to tell her handler she needs a bathroom break.

SPECIAL ABILITY

Horses make everyone let their guard down. We once brought Magic to an assisted-living facility. Magic walked over to a woman in a wheelchair and rested her head in the woman's lap. "Isn't she beautiful," the woman said. "It's a horse!" An employee at the facility immediately started crying. The elderly woman had been living there for three years, and she had never spoken. The woman kept talking after that visit.

MINIATURE HORSES LIVE INTO THEIR 30s. SINCE THERAPY WORK ISN'T PHYSICAL, THEY CAN WORK FOR AS LONG AS THEY ARE HAPPY.

HORSEPOWER VS. HORSE POWER

In the 18th century, James Watt was working on improving the steam engine. Since most of his potential customers relied on horses to pull heavy items, Watt needed a way to explain how many horses his steam engine could replace. So he invented the concept of "horsepower." Unfortunately, this measurement does not actually represent the power of a horse. Instead, it measures the amount of weight that can be moved over a given distance. One horsepower is the equivalent of moving a one-pound (.45 kg) weight 33,000 feet (10,000 m) in one minute. How much horsepower do some modern machines—and people and horses!—have?

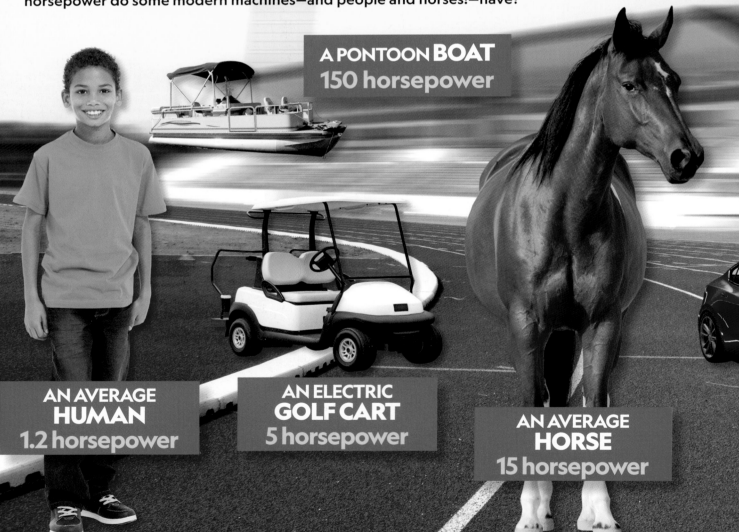

A PONTOON BOAT
150 horsepower

AN AVERAGE HUMAN
1.2 horsepower

AN ELECTRIC GOLF CART
5 horsepower

AN AVERAGE HORSE
15 horsepower

A PASSENGER JET
220,000
horsepower

A SATURN V ROCKET
160 million
horsepower

A SATURN V ROCKET LAUNCHED THE APOLLO MISSIONS THAT FIRST TOOK HUMANS TO THE MOON.

SOME ELECTRIC CARS
430 horsepower

A LARGE DUMP TRUCK
3,500
horsepower

A MODERN LOCOMOTIVE
8,600
horsepower

THE SPEED GENE

IS IT REAL, WHICH HORSES HAVE IT, AND WHAT DOES IT DO?

Did you know that, for horses, speed runs in the family? For thousands of years, humans have partnered the fastest horses with the hope that their horse children would be fast as well. And, in many cases, this was true. Modern scientists think that the reason this works in racehorses is because of the "speed gene," which is a teeny-tiny, can't-even-see-it-with-a-normal-microscope code inside each cell in a horse's body.

READ THE INSTRUCTIONS

Every animal has an instruction manual, called its genome, that tells the cells within its body what to do and how to do it. Horses have 64 chromosomes (KROW-muh-sohms), which are like chapters in their instruction manual. These chromosomes are inherited from their parents. A gene is like one paragraph in the instruction manual. For example, if a cell in a horse's eye needs to know what color the eye should be, it can open the instruction manual (genome), flip to the chapter (chromosome) and then the paragraph (gene) to find the answer.

The problem is that even though the cells know where to look in the instruction manual for answers, humans don't. There is no table of contents.

STEP BY STEP

When humans first read a horse's instruction manual in 2009, it contained 2.7 billion letters. To find the paragraph they cared about, the scientists didn't read every single letter. Rather, they only skimmed sections of each chapter until they found a section that the sprinters shared but the long-distance runners didn't have. They then read each letter of this one section, and finally they found an important difference.

MISSION ACCOMPLISHED

The scientists found that some horses have extra letters in the myostatin (my-oh-STAT-in) gene that dramatically change how fast they can run over a given distance. The myostatin gene provides instructions for muscle growth. Horses with the extra letters in the myostatin gene were the best sprinters. The horses without them ran the best over long distances.

ALL MODERN THOROUGHBREDS CAN TRACE THEIR ANCESTRY TO JUST THREE STALLIONS THAT WERE IMPORTED INTO ENGLAND AROUND 1700.

HUMANS HAVE CHROMOSOMES, JUST LIKE HORSES, BUT WE ONLY HAVE 46.

PONY PUNS

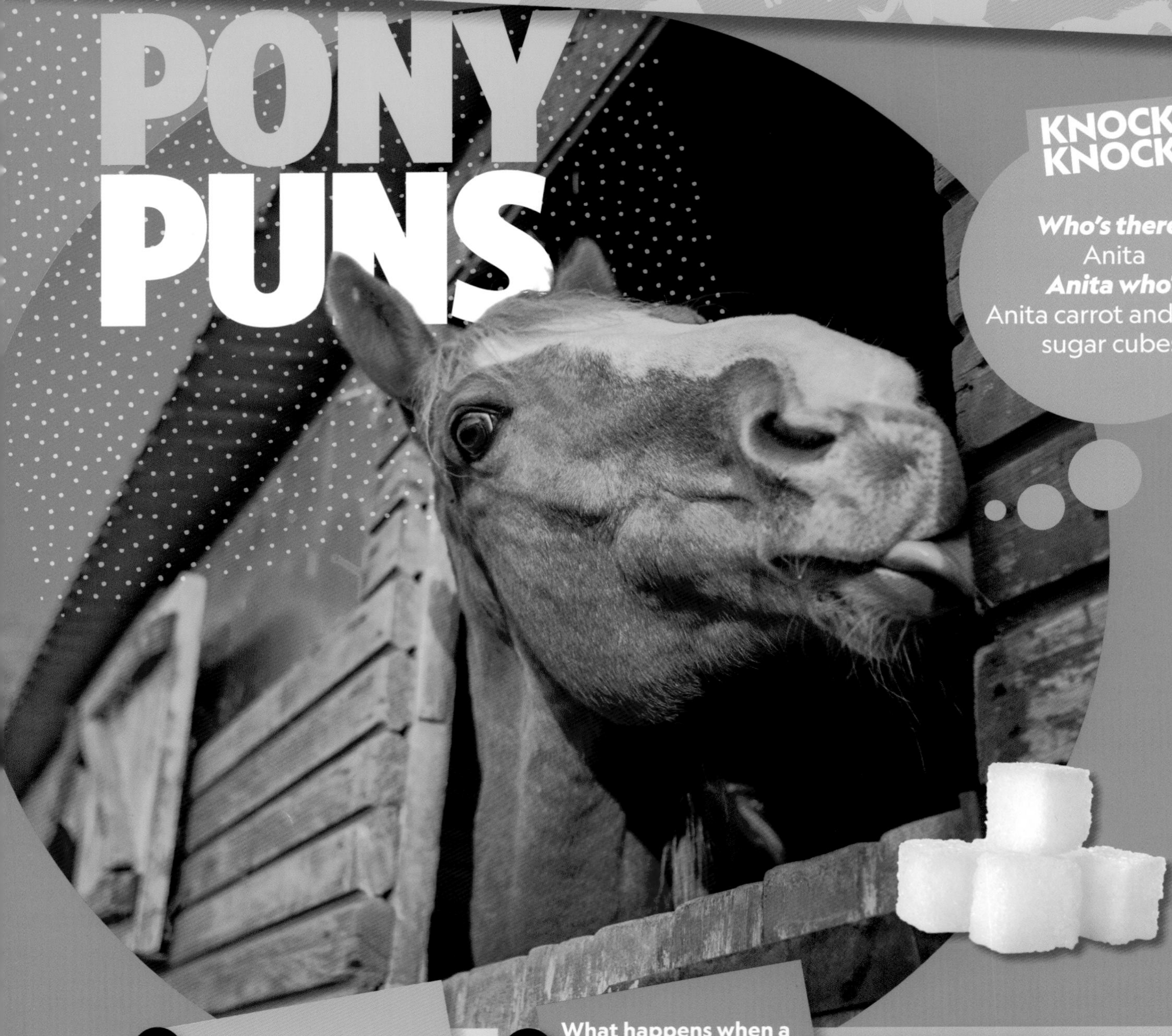

KNOCK, KNOCK.

Who's there?
Anita
Anita who?
Anita carrot and some sugar cubes.

Q Why did the horse put on a sweater?

A He was a little colt.

Q What happens when a white horse jumps into the Black Sea?

A It gets wet!

Q Why do horses live in barns?

A They don't fit in birdhouses.

Q What do you call a horse that likes gardening, knitting, and woodworking?

A A hobby horse.

Q If your horse's nose runs and its feet smell, what is wrong with it?

A It was built upside down.

RIDDLE ME THIS ...

Q A horse named Sam is running in a race. He passes the horse that is in second place. What place is Sam in?

A Second.

HORSES AROUND THE WORLD

The **KAZAKH** people of Kazakhstan use **HORSE MANURE** for things such as **FUEL** and roof insulation.

IN ADDITION TO PULLING THE CARTS THAT TRANSPORT GOODS AROUND THE COUNTRY, **ETHIOPIAN HORSES** ARE USED TO PLAY A GAME CALLED **GUGIS,** WHICH IS SIMILAR TO POLO.

In India, extravagantly dressed horses sometimes carry a **GROOM** to his **WEDDING** ceremony.

In **AMISH** settlements in the United States and Canada, people drive horse-drawn **BUGGIES.**

THE **BEDOUIN** PEOPLE OF THE ARABIAN PENINSULA, NORTHERN AFRICA, AND THE LEVANT CONSIDER SOME ARABIAN HORSES SO PRICELESS THAT THEY CANNOT BE SOLD. THEY CAN ONLY BE GIVEN AS **GIFTS.**

Horses were brought to the island of **HAWAII** to herd cattle. Today, they're mostly used for trail riding and **RODEOS.**

In northern Siberia, one of the coldest places on Earth, the **YAKUT** people ranch with a special breed of horse, the Yakutian. To preserve warmth, the horses never lie down during the winter months. In fact, they enter a state of **"STANDING HIBERNATION"** to conserve energy.

TYPES OF SADDLES

SADDLE UP! HERE ARE SOME HORSE SADDLES FROM AROUND THE WORLD.

ARCTIC OCEAN

Alaska U.S.

NORTH AMERICA

UNITED STATES

PACIFIC OCEAN

ATLANTIC OCEAN

SOUTH AMERICA

Side Saddles

While likely originating in Persia (today's Iran), modern side saddles with three pommels became popular in early-19th-century England and other parts of Europe.

A side saddle allows the rider to ride securely with both legs on one side of the horse.

Contrary to its name, the rider faces forward, not sideways.

The rider's right leg rests between two curved horns, called pommels, and then hangs down the left side of the horse. Her left leg is secured under a third, downward-curving pommel.

These saddles have only one stirrup.

Western Saddles

Western saddles were designed for work rather than fun.

These saddles are bulky and wide to make sure horse and rider are comfortable for long periods of time.

They typically have a horn, which was used when roping cattle. The rider could wrap the rope around the horn to act as a third hand.

Reins are generally held in one hand, which can rest on the horn during long drives.

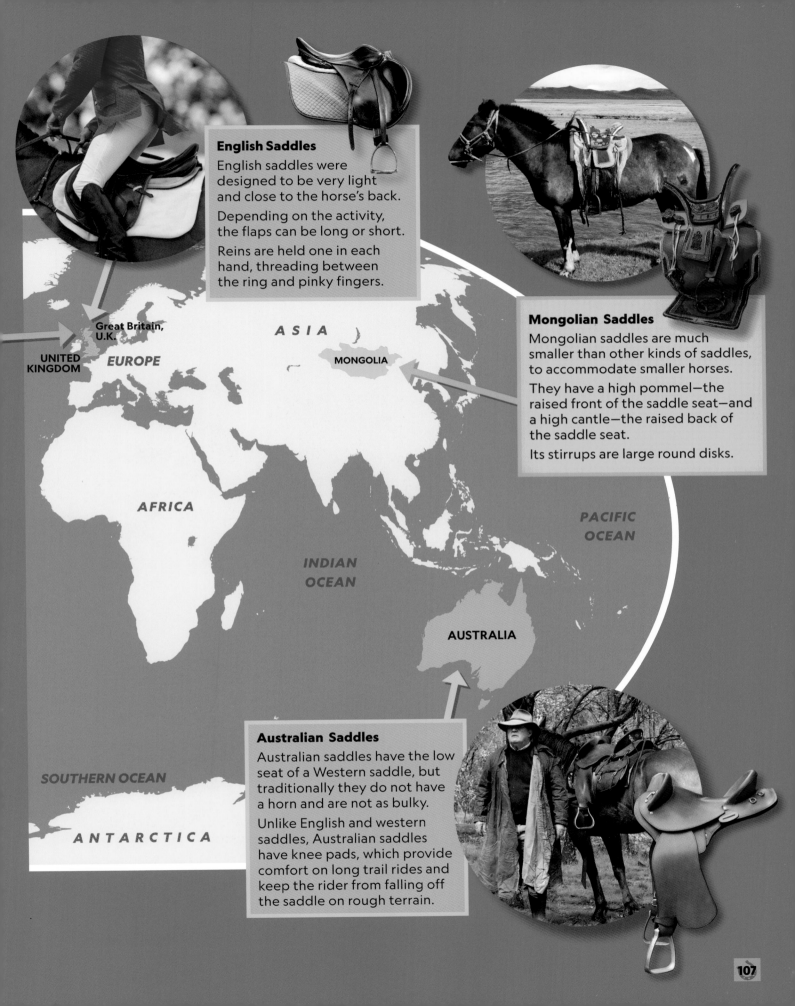

English Saddles

English saddles were designed to be very light and close to the horse's back.

Depending on the activity, the flaps can be long or short.

Reins are held one in each hand, threading between the ring and pinky fingers.

ASIA

Great Britain, U.K.

MONGOLIA

UNITED KINGDOM   **EUROPE**

Mongolian Saddles

Mongolian saddles are much smaller than other kinds of saddles, to accommodate smaller horses.

They have a high pommel—the raised front of the saddle seat—and a high cantle—the raised back of the saddle seat.

Its stirrups are large round disks.

AFRICA

PACIFIC OCEAN

INDIAN OCEAN

AUSTRALIA

SOUTHERN OCEAN

Australian Saddles

Australian saddles have the low seat of a Western saddle, but traditionally they do not have a horn and are not as bulky.

Unlike English and western saddles, Australian saddles have knee pads, which provide comfort on long trail rides and keep the rider from falling off the saddle on rough terrain.

ANTARCTICA

DRAFT HORSES

CHECK OUT THESE GENTLE GIANTS.

BIGGEST OF THE BIG

SHIRE HORSE

While all draft horses are big, Shires tend to be the biggest. These mammoths were historically used to pull barges along canals. Stallions are generally about six feet (1.8 m) tall at the withers, so you might want to bring a ladder!

MOST FAMOUS

CLYDESDALE

Originally from Scotland, Clydesdales were farming horses until tractors replaced them in the 20th century. Today, these majestic steeds appear in parades, pull carriages, and star in Super Bowl commercials.

MOST LIKELY TO WIN AN OSCAR

FRIESIAN

With their sleek, black coats and flowing manes, Friesians have starred in many movies and television shows, including *The Chronicles of Narnia* and *The Hunger Games* film series. Originally from the Friesland province in the Netherlands, Friesians were a popular mount for medieval knights because they were strong enough to carry the heavily armored warriors.

BEST AT PULLING

BELGIAN DRAFT

Originally called the Flemish great horse (named after the region where it originated), the Belgian draft horse regularly wins contests in which horses compete to pull heavy sleds. A pair of Belgians set the world record by pulling 22,000 pounds (9,979 kg) a distance of 5.5 feet (1.7 m).

HEALING HORSES

HIPPOTHERAPY is the use of horseback riding to improve coordination, balance, and strength. In Greek, *hippos* means "horse."

Riding horses can **REDUCE ANXIETY** and release feel-good chemicals, called **ENDORPHINS.**

Hippotherapy can be used to treat children with **CEREBRAL PALSY,** a disorder that affects a child's ability to move or balance. Riding a horse both **STRENGTHENS** muscles needed to walk and helps the brain learn to **BALANCE.**

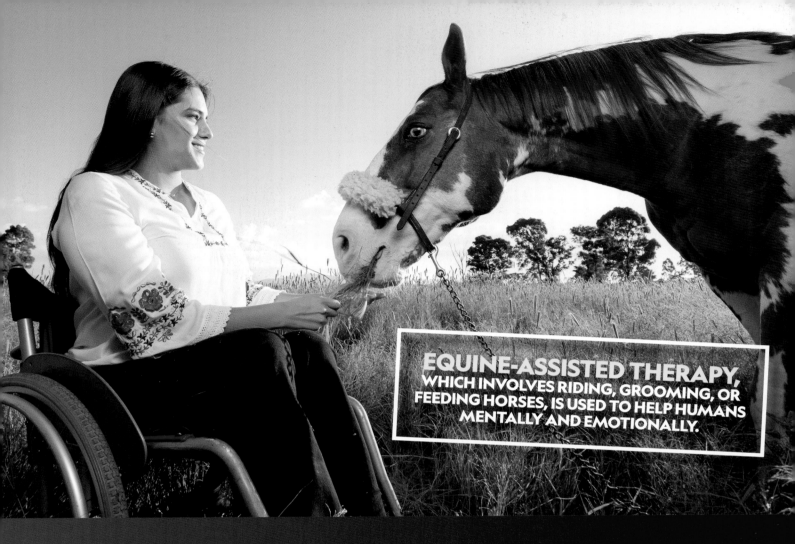

EQUINE-ASSISTED THERAPY, WHICH INVOLVES RIDING, GROOMING, OR FEEDING HORSES, IS USED TO HELP HUMANS MENTALLY AND EMOTIONALLY.

Prison inmates who train wild **MUSTANGS** as part of the **WILD HORSE INMATE PROGRAM** are around **five times less** likely to commit additional crimes in the future.

IN THE 1890s, DOCTORS DISCOVERED THAT THEY COULD USE A TOXIN FROM THE BLOOD OF HORSES TO MAKE AN ANTITOXIN TO STOP A DISEASE IN HUMANS CALLED **DIPHTHERIA.**

HORSE HUMOR

Q What do you call a pony that plays electric guitar?

A A rocking horse.

Q What's the hardest thing about learning to ride a horse?

A The ground!

TONGUE TWISTER

SAY THIS FAST THREE TIMES:

The purple pony pair padded down a pleasant path.

At the end of a long day herding cattle, a cowboy exclaimed, "I'm so hungry, I could eat a horse!" His horse paused, looked up at him, and said, "Quack quack."

YOU'VE GOT TO BE JOKING ...

Q What type of cheese do you use to hide a small horse?

A Mascar-pony.

Q What disease are horses afraid of getting?

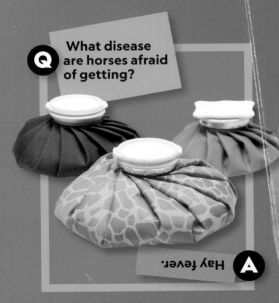

A Hay fever.

THE PALIO OF SIENA, ITALY

FOR 400 YEARS, SIENA HAS HOSTED A HORSE RACE IN THE MIDDLE OF ITS CITY. About one week before the race, thousands of pounds of clay are carted in to fashion a track in the town square. For all this effort, the race lasts only about a minute, and the prize is a simple silk flag. So why does life in Siena revolve around the Palio (pronounced PAL-ee-oh)?

THE NEIGHBORHOODS

Siena is divided into 17 neighborhoods, each with its own mascot. Ten of these neighborhoods compete in each horse race, one held in July and the other in August. The Sienese view their neighborhood as an extension of their family. The neighborhoods have their own museums, churches, and social clubs. They have their own songs, cheers, and colors. Birthdays, holidays, and special occasions are celebrated with one's neighbors. The Palio is a celebration of these neighborhoods. In the four-day festival before each race, hundreds of people parade around the city in elaborate costumes as drummers beat a tune, oxen pull chariots, and flag wavers throw their colorful flags high into the air. The neighborhoods cheer at the twice-daily practice races and celebrate with feasts every night.

THE FLAG

Originally, the word "palio" did not refer to the race itself but instead to the silk flag that the winner received as a prize. In fact, 400 years before the horse race took on its current form, the neighborhoods of Siena held festivals in the town square, with people competing in a variety of games to win a silk flag.

IF A RIDER FALLS OFF HIS HORSE IN THE PALIO, THE HORSE CAN STILL WIN THE RACE IF IT FINISHES FIRST.

IN THE PALIO, COMPETITORS WOULD RATHER FINISH LAST THAN SECOND. THE LAST-PLACE FINISHER NEVER HAD A CHANCE. THE SECOND-PLACE FINISHER ALMOST WON BUT DIDN'T, AND SO IS CONSIDERED THE FIRST LOSER.

TASTY TREATS

While horses can survive on a diet of mostly hay and water, every equine needs a cheat day! Here's a healthy no-bake treat that you can make for that special pony in your life.

PEPPERMINT COOKIES
MAKES 4–6 TREATS

INGREDIENTS:
1 CUP OF ROLLED OATS
¼ CUP OF WATER (ADD MORE IF THE MIXTURE IS TOO DRY)
1 TABLESPOON OF MOLASSES
6 PEPPERMINTS

MAKE SURE YOU CONSULT A VETERINARIAN BEFORE FEEDING YOUR HORSE ANY KIND OF SUGARY TREAT. WHILE MANY HORSES LOVE AND DO WELL WITH PEPPERMINTS, SOME HORSES HAVE TROUBLE DIGESTING SWEETS.

STEP 1:
Mix the oats and water until combined.

STEP 2:
Add the molasses and stir. The mixture should stick together like cookie dough.

STEP 3:
Take a small handful and roll it into a ball.

STEP 4:
Press one peppermint into the center of each ball.

STEP 5:
Place each treat on a plate or cookie sheet.

STEP 6:
Put them in the refrigerator until they harden.

THE APPALOOSA IS NAMED AFTER THE

PALOUSE RIVER VALLEY

IN WASHINGTON STATE, U.S.A.,

WHICH IS WHERE THE

NEZ PERCE

INDIANS

DEVELOPED THE BREED.

THE APPALOOSA IS THE ONLY HORSE BREED WHOSE SCLERA (THE WHITE PORTION OF THE EYE) IS ALWAYS VISIBLE.

TRIVIA TROT

HAVE YOU PICKED UP ANY EQUINE TRIVIA ALONG THIS OLD DUSTY TRAIL? YOU'RE ABOUT TO FIND OUT! WRITE YOUR ANSWERS ON A SEPARATE PIECE OF PAPER AND THEN CHECK THE ANSWER KEY BELOW. IF YOU CAN'T FIGURE OUT AN ANSWER, LOOK BACK THROUGH THE SECOND HALF OF THE BOOK.

1 When a horse lifts one diagonal pair of feet followed by the other diagonal pair of feet, it is ___ .

   a. walking

   b. skipping

   c. hopping

   d. trotting

2 What is the only breed of horse whose sclera (the white portion of the eye) is always visible?

   a. zorse

   b. Appaloosa

   c. Belgian Draft

   d. Arabian

3 How long ago were horses first domesticated?

   a. six million years ago

   b. six hundred years ago

   c. six thousand years ago

   d. six billion years ago

4 Why can you lead a horse to water but not make it drink?

   a. Horses are stubborn.

   b. Horses that sweat a lot don't know they are thirsty.

   c. Horses cannot see water.

   d. Horses can only drink when no one else is around.

5 When a horse is angry, it will ___ .

   a. pin its ears against its head

   b. point its ears at the thing it is mad at

   c. swivel its ears back and forth like a princess wave

   d. cover its ears with its hooves

6 True or False?

Miniature therapy horses are trained to stomp their front foot to tell their handler they need to go to the restroom.

9 According to myth, drinking from a unicorn horn can ___.

a. cure any illness

b. quench any thirst

c. make water taste like strawberries

d. poison the drinker

10 The Greek word for horse is ___.

a. biblio

b. hippos

c. logos

d. tropos

7 A group of wild horses traveling together is called a ___.

a. herd

b. harem

c. band

d. all of the above

8 Alexander the Great tamed an untamable horse by ___.

a. giving it a carrot

b. blindfolding it

c. pointing its head away from its shadow

d. singing it a song

ANSWERS: 1. d; 2. b; 3. c; 4. b; 5. a; 6. True; 7. d; 8. c; 9. a; 10. b

FIND OUT MORE

Want to rein in more info about horses? Check out these books, and ask a grown-up to help you explore these fascinating websites and incredible explorers.

BOOKS

Gallop! 100 Fun Facts About Horses by Kitson Jazynka, National Geographic Kids, 2018.

National Geographic Readers: Ponies by Laura Marsh, National Geographic Kids, 2011.

Ponies and Horses Sticker Activity Book. National Geographic Kids, 2015.

Puzzle Book: Horses and Ponies. National Geographic, 2019.

ONLINE RESOURCES

Gentle Carousel Miniature Therapy Horses

Horse page at Britannica Kids

National Geographic Kids

Przewalski's Horse page at Smithsonian National Zoo

EXPLORERS

An explorer is someone who takes their work out into the field to learn more about it. They research questions, make observations, and report what they discover.

Benjamin Arbuckle, archaeologist and researcher

Sylvia Johnson, documentary filmmaker

Barbara Promberger, biologist and equestrian ecotourism organizer

Kenneth D. Rose, paleontologist

William T. Taylor, archaeologist and researcher

Arabian horse

INDEX

CREDITS

ACKNOWLEDGMENTS

FOR EVA, GREY, AXEL, AND HAZEL, WHO FORCE ME TO GALLOP BUT MAKE IT FEEL LIKE A TROT. —N.C.C.

Since 1888, the National Geographic Society has funded more than 14,000 research, conservation, education, and storytelling projects around the world. National Geographic Partners distributes a portion of the funds it receives from your purchase to National Geographic Society to support programs including the conservation of animals and their habitats. To learn more, visit natgeo.com/info.

For more information, visit nationalgeographic.com, call 1-877-873-6846, or write to the following address:

National Geographic Partners, LLC
1145 17th Street NW
Washington, DC 20036-4688 U.S.A.

For librarians and teachers: nationalgeographic.com/books/librarians-and-educators

More for kids from National Geographic: natgeokids.com

National Geographic Kids magazine inspires children to explore their world with fun yet educational articles on animals, science, nature, and more. Using fresh storytelling and amazing photography, *Nat Geo Kids* shows kids ages 6 to 14 the fascinating truth about the world—and why they should care. natgeo.com/subscribe

For rights or permissions inquiries, please contact National Geographic Books Subsidiary Rights: bookrights@natgeo.com

Designed by Rachael Hamm Plett, Moduza Design

Trade paperback ISBN: 978-1-4263-7391-6
Reinforced library binding ISBN: 978-1-4263-7436-4

The publisher would like to thank the team that made this book possible: Shelby Lees and Ariane Szu-Tu, editors; Grace Hill Smith, project editor; Sarah J. Mock, senior photo editor; Michelle Harris, fact-checker; Kari Turner, professor and equine extension specialist, University of Georgia, for her expert review; and Lauren Sciortino and David Marvin, associate designers.

Printed in South Korea
23/SPSK/1